A
TWO-FACED
PRESS?

A Twentieth Century Fund Paper

A
Two-Faced
Press?

BY TOM GOLDSTEIN

PP Priority Press Publications / New York / 1986

The Twentieth Century Fund is an independent research foundation which undertakes policy studies of economic, political, and social institutions and issues. The Fund was founded in 1919 and endowed by Edward A. Filene.

Foreword

Freedom of the press, enshrined in the First Amendment, is one of the glories of American democracy. Most of the press takes its freedom seriously, which is to say that it acts responsibly in seeking to provide fair and accurate news coverage and editorial commentary. A press that is free, though, also is a press that can be irresponsible, acting unfairly or distortedly. That is the price we pay for freedom. If it is sometimes a high price, it has never been so high that it put freedom in jeopardy. To the contrary, irresponsible journals have sometimes proved invaluable in questioning and exposing authority. While many Americans get annoyed or angry at the press, responsible or irresponsible, from time to time, none of us would shackle press freedom.

Tom Goldstein, a journalist and scholar of journalism, who is the author of *The News At Any Cost*, questions whether that freedom extends to a newspaper's advertising columns. He is especially concerned about the prevailing practice of the responsible press to give full news coverage to products that may be harmful to consumers and editorially warn against the dangers of such products, but then accept advertising from their purveyors. Goldstein sees a need for greater social responsibility, especially by the responsible press, that would deny advertising space to such advertisers.

Goldstein's position is both novel and controversial. As an institution that has long had an interest in public policy issues concerning the press, the Twentieth Century Fund thought that it merited an airing. In doing so, we are not endorsing his views. However, we think that he has raised a number of interesting questions about the nature and extent of press freedom: Does press freedom cover advertising? Is a newspaper playing fair with its readers by accepting advertising for potentially harmful products? Is a newspaper's credibility at stake when its editorials support, say, action to restrict or eliminate cigarette smoking while its advertising pages suggest that there is something glamorous or satisfying about smoking? Can a newspaper decide to follow a selective policy, banning some potentially harmful advertisers but not others? And if it is agreed that some advertising should be banned as harmful, how can such action be enforced?

Quite apart from these questions, Goldstein's account makes clear that responsible papers, including the very best, fall short of the idealistic notions that we like to think motivates a free press. But that should not be surprising. They are, to begin with, business corporations with a need to operate profitably. They are run by fallible individuals who, it must be admitted, are adept at exercising their critical faculties about other institutions or individuals but do not take kindly to criticism.

The press has a number of valid responses to Goldstein's view of their obligations. At the very least then, his commentary should stir up debate about the limits, if any, to press freedom. It may also lead newspaper managements to review their current policies and practices. If they do, they may consider closing the gap between what they preach and what they sell.

M. J. Rossant, DIRECTOR
The Twentieth Century Fund
September 1986

Contents

Acknowledgments

I wish to acknowledge the invaluable research assistance of Lonn Johnston and the keen editorial advice of Joe Spieler and Evan Cornog.

Tom Goldstein
Acting Professor
Graduate School of Journalism,
University of California, Berkeley

Preface

All advertising of tobacco should be banned by law, the American Medical Association has proposed....We wonder what the good doctors were smoking when they approved that policy.

—Editorial, *Des Moines Register*, December 18, 1985

This paper examines how the advertising policies of newspapers and magazines conform to—and diverge from—the idea of social responsibility held by these publications. It was prompted by a resolution passed in December 1985 by the American Medical Association (AMA) urging "the adoption of legislation that would ban the advertising of tobacco products." Earlier in the year, a coalition of activists representing education, religious, and public health groups had mounted an effort to ban advertising of beer and wine on television—similar to the ban of tobacco advertising on television. Thus, it is an opportune time to explore the difficult questions raised by attempts to control what the media present.

Even though the issues in terms of print and broadcast media differ substantially, what is similar is that those advocating the restriction of cigarette and alcohol advertising have asked Congress to deal with an anomaly. They want Congress to restrict the marketing and promotion of products while allowing their production and consumption.

On this point, the tobacco industry, which historically has been skillful in lobbying Congress for price supports and other legislation, has teamed up with publishers who have a dual in-

1

terest in the proposal—freedom of the press would be adversely affected by such a ban and revenues of most publications would suffer if the AMA proposal were enacted. At stake in the AMA resolution is $2.6 billion in annual tobacco advertising revenues: 9 percent of all magazine advertising and 1 percent of newspaper advertising comes from tobacco companies.

Moreover, tobacco is thought by many to be inherently harmful; and alcohol, if abused, is harmful not only to consumers but to other parties as well. These products have special characteristics, but the policy debate surrounding them extends to other potentially harmful products and raises broader questions: Should any curbs—legal or voluntary—be placed on the advertising of lawful products? Does doing so interfere with the freedom of the press? Is public skepticism of the press fostered by the apparent conflict of newspapers' accepting advertisements for a product that editorials attack? Can we have a press that behaves as a good citizen and yet sustains itself commercially?

To examine these issues I will draw upon dozens of interviews with publishers and editors and upon the 110 responses to a questionnaire on advertising acceptability policies that I mailed to 165 publishers and advertising managers of newspapers and magazines. In addition, many publishers provided invaluable clippings and internal documents.

What has emerged is a mosaic of seeming inconsistencies:

• Most newspapers say one thing on their editorial pages about smoking and take a contradictory position when it comes to their advertising columns.
• Many publishers say they accept cigarette advertisements because the maker of any legal product has a "right" to advertise, yet some of these publishers systematically, or capriciously, exclude certain advertisers.
• Publishers righteously cry foul when the threat of government intervention is mentioned, yet many blur the distinction between a law banning advertising of a harmful substance and voluntary action on their part.

By examining proposals to control advertising, I hope to contribute to the debate over whether publishers should as a matter of consistency and social conscience—without being forced to by the government—refuse to accept certain advertising.

1 / The Responsibility of the Press

One can support the right of access for advertising and still shake one's head in disapproval of the exercise of that right. . . .

—Editorial, *The Christian Science Monitor,*
December 12, 1985

In 1982, at a conference on "The Responsibilities of Journalists," Leonard Silk, economics columnist of *The New York Times,* asked: "Can a newspaper simultaneously be both a business serving its own interest and affect to be a quasi-public institution serving everybody's best interests, as defined by the newspaper itself?" In his speech at the conference, at the University of Notre Dame, Silk also observed: "I don't think anybody in his right mind believes that a great newspaper's purpose is just to make money or that its greatness is defined by how much money it makes."

Yet these days newspapers seem preoccupied with profits. This is reflected in the images of financial success that appear in the 1985 annual reports of many publicly held newspaper companies. The language of these reports is disconcertingly far removed from any notion of high-minded service to the public that practicing journalists might hold. With the caveat that annual reports are designed to please the corporation's stockholders, a look at some annual reports sheds light on what publishers think is important.

The cover of The New York Times Company's 1985 annual report simply says: "We reached across the nation during another year of record earnings." On the first page of the report, the two chief officers of the company, Arthur Ochs Sulzberger and Walter E. Mattson, properly remind shareholders that "size is but one measure of a company, and scarcely the most important." More important, they write, is "being a company that is synonymous with the accomplishment of excellence." Then, instead of speaking about the high quality of the newspaper the company publishes, they immediately tick off a series of financial indicators, such as higher net income and increases in cash flow, that reflect the company's growth.

Dominating the cover of The Washington Post Company's report is an arresting black-and-white, head-and-shoulders photograph of Joel Chaseman, president of Post-Newsweek Stations. Underneath his photograph is this quote: "We try to factor the economic equation so that immediate actions and investments serve longer-term designs. . . ." Most of the report is devoted to statements of four senior managers who "examine some key issues affecting our business today and tomorrow." Only a few paragraphs in the report are devoted to editorial comment on the company's two major operations, the *Washington Post* newspaper and *Newsweek* magazine.

A major Washington Post stockholder is Berkshire Hathaway, Inc., an Omaha, Nebraska conglomerate. In the company's chatty and informative annual report, Warren E. Buffett, its chairman and one of the most astute investors in the country, reviewed the year 1985 for Berkshire Hathaway shareholders. He lavished praise on Katherine Graham, the chief executive officer of The Washington Post Co., noting her "stunning business success." He told his shareholders that he intended to hold "indefinitely" whatever Post stock was legally possible because the company was bound to grow and because "we know that management is both able and shareholder-oriented."

Early in 1985, in the *Wall Street Journal*, the journalist Hodding Carter III, a former newspaper executive, wondered whether the industry is so dominated by those "acutely sensitive to its business necessities that it will slight the mission for which it was given constitutional protection."

With publishers seemingly so preoccupied with profits, what happens to the underlying purposes of publishing? In the past, many of the heroes of journalism were those who acted against their immediate economic interest. For example, Hodding Carter's father, as editor and publisher of the *Delta-Democrat Times* in Greenville, Mississippi, was one of a handful of

Southern journalists who put principle ahead of profit in the 1950s and early 1960s. They favored integration, and they ran their editorials saying so on page one. They were unpopular in their communities. Their papers were boycotted by readers— and by advertisers. They lost money. Their deeds serve as a reminder that publishers have not always been in business merely to turn out a handsome balance sheet.

A quarter of a century ago, no newspaper stock was traded on the public exchanges. Now, the ten largest newspapers and most other major papers are publicly held. Public ownership does carry special responsibilities, but where does management's obligation to please shareholders leave the reader?

The Roles of Publishers

Leonard Silk, in his speech at Notre Dame, said that "the aim is not just making money but is also essentially the same as the business of a university: truth-seeking, truth-telling."

Silk's comparison of a newspaper to a university echoes what Robert Maynard Hutchins wrote in 1948:

> If the purpose of a university is to have a lot of students, then the university that has the most is the best. If the purpose of a newspaper is to make a lot of money, then the newspaper that makes the most is the best. If, however, the purpose of universities and newspapers is the same, to the extent that both should aim at public enlightenment, then largeness and profit become irrelevant.

The thoughts expressed by Silk and Hutchins seem oddly Pollyannaish in a day when most newspapers are parts of large corporations and are modeled after their parent companies— not universities. In a world in which profits are critical, there are three ways in which publishers customarily try to exercise their social responsibility:

• They act as corporate citizens of the communities they serve. Whatever motivates them—philanthropy, self-promotion, or enlightened self-interest—publishers as individuals play a number of roles in their communities. They serve on the boards of nonprofit organizations, they help with the renovation of decaying inner cities, they provide scholarships, they sponsor athletic contests, and they boost their cities.

• They oversee the advertising that appears in their newspapers.

• They finance the editorial side of their newspapers. This permits the press to fulfill its role as observer, watchdog, adversary, agenda-setter. The larger the editorial budget, presumably the better the publication.

The Publisher as Corporate Citizen

Ordinarily, rather than exercise their responsibility in their advertising policies, where conscience can result in lost profits, publishers prefer to demonstrate their social responsibility where the results are visible—in their communities. Most often, what is good for the community is also financially beneficial for the owners of the paper. A bustling community without strife is a welcome home to businesses, which in turn advertise and support a newspaper.

But the community activity of publishers also poses problems. It can place reporters and editors in a difficult position when they do an important part of their job—scrutinizing civic activities. For example, for many years, until he was forced out in 1983 by directors of the company that owned Minneapolis's *Star* and *Tribune*, John Cowles, Jr., served as both a very active president of the company and a civic leader. He was instrumental in building local cultural institutions, and he led a coalition of business leaders and public officials that forged links with the minority community.

He also took the lead in promoting a domed stadium in downtown Minneapolis, and he personally contributed nearly $5 million to the project. That smacked of a conflict of interest to the journalists who worked for him, and forty-five of them took out an advertisement, which—to its credit—the *Tribune* ran:

> As journalists, our responsibility is to be dispassionate and fair in covering public issues. Our role is to report, not to participate in these issues. Because we work for the *Minneapolis Tribune,* we recognize some people may question our fidelity to that principle when John Cowles, Jr. . . . is a leading advocate in the debate over whether and where the sports stadium should be built. We bought this advertisement to assure our readers that our professional principles have not been undermined by Cowles' involvement in the stadium issue. We neither advocate nor oppose building a stadium, domed or un-domed, at any location. Furthermore, neither Cowles nor any other company executive has tried to influence the *Tribune's* coverage of this issue. But to prevent even an appearance of such a conflict of interest, we believe management should avoid a leadership role in sensitive political and economic issues.

Cowles's involvement distorted the coverage the issue received. The editor of the *Star*, which subsequently was merged into the *Tribune*, recalled that his staff had to bend over backwards in its coverage. "The greatest contribution an owner can make to his community is by putting out a quality newspaper that has a high standard of integrity and ethics," Stephen Isaacs, editor of the *Star*, said in an interview with Gene Goodwin, a journalism professor at Pennsylvania State University. In another interview with Goodwin, Cowles disagreed and argued that publishers "have a positive obligation to engage in the important activities of the community." Publishers, he said, "should be able to express their views not just through their editorial pages but through their efforts and work in the community."

Although I am unaware of any other group of journalists bold enough to take out an advertisement embarrassing the owner of their paper, this debate has been repeated in newsrooms across the country. Working journalists—many of whom are governed by stringent codes restricting their outside activities—are pitted against their bosses. While the journalists may score debating points, ordinarily the bosses prevail.

More so than most others, the proprietors of the *Dallas Morning News* act on their belief that a journalistic enterprise must assume certain obligations to the community. In its 1985 annual report, A. H. Belo Corporation, owner of *The Morning News* and other media properties, trumpets the newspaper's involvement with the outside world. Six consecutive pages are filled with handsome pictures of the company's directors. One is a managing partner of Trammell Crow Company, the developer. Another is a partner of Goldman, Sachs & Co., the investment banking house. A third is chairman of the board of a local savings and loan association.

These directors represent another possible conflict-of-interest problem. Each has business interests that the newspaper must cover in its news columns. This places the journalists who must cover these companies in an awkward, perhaps untenable position. But few publishers speak out against this. An exception is Loren Ghiglione, editor and publisher of two small newspapers, the *Bristol* (Connecticut) *Press* and the *Southbridge* (Massachusetts) *News*. He argues that outside directors—people not employed by or closely connected with the papers—do not belong on their boards. Papers, he says, can "survive quite easily without outside directors—and could thereby eliminate an area of apparent conflict of interest." His argument has great appeal—except that he, like Hutchins, is nobly naive. Newspapers follow the corporate model, where the existence of outside directors is generally not challenged.

But the other, more publicly discussed, conflict of interest involves the role in the community of those who run the papers. At the *Dallas Morning News*, the officers of the company are also active in community affairs; they have taken positions of leadership in organizations that help the zoo, the opera, a local hospital, the YMCA, the area's parks, and its troubled youths.

These are the kinds of civic activities that earn executives undiluted praise if they are involved in just about any business other than journalism. This contradiction goes to the heart of what a newspaper is. Some journalists, like Isaacs, believe that the greatest contribution that publishers can make to a community is putting out a quality newspaper. Others, like Cowles and Joe Dealey, who recently retired as chairman of A. H. Belo, feel that there is an additional obligation to engage in community service. In a 1983 commencement address, Dealey said:

> It is necessary [for a newspaper] to give real evidence to its living being by taking an active role in community affairs beyond the mere remarking of such and such condition or project. To do this requires that employees to an extent reasonable and practical get out in the hustings and rub elbows with persons involved in important and worthwhile civic endeavors such as needed hospital capital programs, Red Cross drives, the United Way, the arts, etc. It is even better when the owners and operators take on major responsibilities in these efforts. This sort of essential dynamism places the newspaper in the forefront and greatly tends to diminish thinking that it sits merely as a judge of affairs or tally counter of results.

Limitations on the "Freedom to Advertise"

Through their advertising pages, publishers match buyers and sellers of goods. Advertising is the engine that drives the news. With few exceptions, the size of a newspaper depends not on the day's news, but on the day's advertising. Most newspapers and magazines derive between two-thirds and three-quarters of their revenues from advertisers.

In response to my questionnaire, publishers most often said that they accepted all tasteful advertisements.* Many couched

---

*For a more detailed examination of the questions involved in determining acceptability, see chapter 3.

their decision to do so in the language of the law, sometimes arguing—erroneously—that they have what amounts to a constitutional obligation to accept advertising. Only a few said that it was in their best economic interest to do so. But although most publishers say that they take a hands-off approach to advertising, and many say that they should accept advertising for any legal product, some publishers are very picky about what advertising appears, especially advertising dealing with sexually suggestive material. This is one area where publishers are willing to sacrifice profits to principle. For example, the *Arizona Republic* gave up $10,000 in revenues because it refused to accept advertisements for "Bolero," the X-rated movie starring Bo Derek.

To an extent, a paper's concern with community is reflected in its policy regarding advertising. Some papers set down written guidelines. For example, *The Dallas Morning News* has a five-page pamphlet, "Advertising Standards of Acceptability in *The Dallas Morning News*," which begins by saying the standards set forth "have been formulated not only for the protection of the reader, but also the advertiser. The good names and reputations of honest businesses should not be jeopardized by those who ignore or bend the truth."

The newspaper refuses to accept advertisements that contain "statements of doubtful honesty," advertisements "in bad taste or offensive to any group on moral, religious or discriminatory grounds," or advertisements that "contain suggestive captions or illustrations." The newspaper also says that advertising "likely to cause injury to the health" of the reader is unacceptable. (This was the only advertising code of several dozen that I looked at which contained such language.) But Dial Amos, assistant retail manager of the newspaper, said that he could not recall any product falling in this category that the newspaper had rejected. He said the phrase was not broad enough to include cigarette advertising.

Taking a Stand

One of the best indications of how publications view their social responsibility is their reaction to the 1985 AMA proposal to ban cigarette advertising, a proposal that would cost them advertising dollars but presumably would lead to a physically healthier community. The exact number of editorials written about the AMA proposal is impossible to pin down, but using a variety of sources, including the AMA clipping service, the clipping service of a major tobacco company, and my questionnaire, I could locate only three dozen editorials that discussed the ban. That represents about 2 percent of the daily newspapers in the country. In addition to the editorials, about two dozen columnists, some of them widely syndicated, commented on the AMA proposal.

Predictably, where it was commented on, the AMA proposal was inhospitably received. "The nation's press has greeted the proposal with an enthusiasm generally reserved for letter bombs," wrote Donald Kaul, a columnist for the *Philadelphia Daily News*. Most editorials and columns derided the proposal and fell back on the comfortable—but disingenuous—notion that products that can be legally sold are entitled to be advertised. The proposal raised few editorial doubts and led to little soul-searching, at least publicly. There were the obligatory news stories for a day or two, but there was little follow-up or analysis. Many of the stories, editorials, and columns were riddled with inaccuracies and distortions.

Editorial writers and columnists generally treated those advocating restrictions on cigarette advertising—the AMA, the American Heart Association, the American Cancer Society, the National Advisory Council of Drug Abuse, the American Public Health Association—as bothersome cranks. Overwhelmingly, though, for several years editorials have condemned smoking, which is blamed for at least 350,000, and perhaps as many as 500,000, deaths each year.

Some editorials written in reaction to the AMA proposal suggested that the use of tobacco be curbed by increasing taxes on cigarettes or by reducing subsidies to the tobacco industry or by establishing smoke-free areas. Some papers were sympathetic to the goals of the AMA and the other groups. The *Buffalo News* said the "doctors' proposal has the worthy aim of discouraging smoking." The *Chicago Sun Times* endorsed the AMA's "relentless educational campaign." The *Gainesville Sun* pleaded "mea culpa," saying that "we share the AMA's vision of a smokeless society"—and yet the newspaper gave every indication that it would continue its policy of accepting cigarette advertising.

Of those editorials, only one, in the *Deseret News* of Salt Lake City, endorsed the AMA plan, and one other, in the *Christian Science Monitor*, suggested that voluntary restraint on the part of the press might be preferable to the proposed legislation. Several successful magazines, including *Reader's Digest* and

Good Housekeeping, have refused cigarette advertisements. ("We will not promote products that can destroy lives," the *Reader's Digest* said in a statement to *Common Cause Magazine* in 1986. "It's a costly principle. We figure that we've relinquished some $242.5 million in potential revenue over the past 30 years.")

Other than the *Monitor* and the *Deseret News*—publications that have strong connections with churches opposed to smoking—only a handful of small newspapers reject cigarette advertisements. One is the *Journal* of Salina, Kansas, with a daily circulation of 30,000, which discontinued all national cigarette advertising in 1984. "It was a little hard to justify in my mind that we editorialize in opposition to smoking and then turn around and accept the revenue that was generated from accepting cigarette advertising," said Fred Vandergrift, the paper's publisher.

That most newspapers regularly campaign against smoking on their editorial pages while accepting advertisements to help sell tobacco products leads to a "split-level ethical house"—a phrase employed by Clifford Christians, Kim Rotzoll, and Mark Fackler in *Media Ethics: Cases and Moral Reasoning*. Editorial writers tell the readers what is good for them, and most take the position that smoking decidedly is not. The advertising side adopts a laissez-faire attitude and sells space to cigarette makers. If products are legal, they argue, information should be supplied so that individuals can exercise their own judgment.

Publishers of the major publications explain this seeming inconsistency by saying that the editorial and business sides of newspapers are divided like church and state, that a Chinese wall separates them. That is, the editorial people can bite the advertising hand that feeds them, but the acceptance of advertising should never be dictated by an editorial position.

Breaching the Chinese Wall

The real world is not that neat; the separation of the business side from the news and editorial sides of a publication is far from absolute. In his book, *Goodbye Gutenberg*, Anthony Smith, now the director of the British Film Institute, traces the history of American newspapers. He argues that there can be no absolute distinction in "the ways in which the content of a paper is coded for the reader—as news, as comment, or as advertisement." In one society, for example, "the announcement that a ship is arriving or departing is news; in another it is read as an advertisement. The fact that a large corporation is seeking a new top executive is news, whereas its search for a dozen lathe operators would be the subject of a paid advertisement."

Over the years, the Chinese wall between the advertising and the editorial sides has hardly been impenetrable. In his book, *Media Monopoly*, Ben Bagdikian, dean of the Graduate School of Journalism at Berkeley, notes that as recently as 1950, "it was common for newspapers to resist news that offended a major advertiser. Department store fires, safety violations in stores, public health actions against restaurants that advertised, and lawsuits against car dealers seldom made their way into print."

The same seems to be true in the case of cigarette advertising; there is considerable anecdotal evidence that cigarette advertising affects coverage of smoking—a proposition that is almost ritually denied by publishers. Not one of the 110 newspaper and magazine publishers who responded to my questionnaire could—or would—cite an instance where an advertiser had influenced news coverage about cigarettes.

For decades, though, journalists have suspected that news about the harmful properties of cigarettes has not been fully covered. In 1935, in *Freedom of the Press*, Georges Seldes, the press critic, complained that newspapers suppressed stories about the dangers of cigarettes. In the midst of a Lucky Strike campaign, "Reach for a Lucky instead of a sweet," a learned friend of Seldes made this statement on behalf of the Medical Association of New York: "Excessive use of tobacco to kill the appetite is a double-edged sword, for nicotine poisoning and starvation both leave dire results in their trail." This, commented Seldes, "apparently was not news," for no newspaper had a story about it.

Evidence of influence continues to be discussed anecdotally. In a 2,500-word article in the *Washington Post* in December 1985, reporter Susan Okie documented "a widespread perception among writers, editors and antismoking organizations that cigarette advertising is influencing the news Americans read about smoking." Okie found that the health effects of smoking are especially "played down in many women's magazines that accept cigarette advertising."

In 1984, one of the most celebrated cases of such influence arose when an article on cigarettes assigned by *The New Republic* to David Owen, a free-lance writer, was suppressed. Owen said the article was spiked by Martin Peretz, the magazine's publisher, who told him that "this is a costly crusade that I am willing to forego." Peretz said that he killed the story because he thought it was "hysterical." "I myself can't judge what is medically sound," he said, but "I thought it was journalistically inflammatory and therefore not illuminating in any serious way." Owen's article was subsequently purchased by *The Washington Monthly*, a magazine that does not accept cigarette advertisements.

Ultimately, though, it is not possible to document fully cases in which cigarette advertising has influenced the play of stories. In many cases, it just may be that editors are inured to the health dangers and do not see these stories as news. Dr. William Bennett, editor of the *Harvard Medical School Health Letter*, recently commented:

> The public doesn't like to think about the cigarette problem. And, because the victims die one-by-one in hospital beds instead of all at once in crashes or episodes of mass poisoning, the cigarette crisis is not "news."

A Model from the Past

Nearly a hundred years ago, *The Ladies Home Journal*, edited by Edward Bok, announced it would no longer accept advertisements for patent medicines. "It was a pioneer stroke," recalled Bok in his Pulitzer Prize-winning autobiography, *The Americanization of Edward Bok*, published in 1920. Bok went on to say that in the two years following his 1892 decision, seven other newspapers and periodicals followed suit:

> The American people were slaves to self-medication, and the patent-medicine makers had it all their own way. There was little or no legal regulation as to the ingredients in their nostrums; the mails were wide open to circulars, and the pages of even the most reputable periodicals welcomed their advertisements. The patent medicine business in the United States ran into the hundreds of millions of dollars annually.

In addition to refusing to accept such advertisements, Bok, with several other muckrakers, including Mark Sullivan and Samuel Hopkins Adams, wrote articles exposing the claims of the popular "cure-alls," many of which were harmful substances. During his campaign against these nostrums, Bok once used an advertisement out of a newspaper that ended with this statement: "Mrs. Pinkham, in her laboratory at Lynn, Massachusetts, is able to do more for the ailing of women of America than the family physician. . . ." Next to this, Bok placed a photograph of Mrs. Pinkham's tombstone, showing that she had died twenty-two years earlier. "It was one of the most effective pieces of copy that the magazine used," Bok recalled.

Bok wrote about the effects of his efforts: "Reputable newspapers and magazines were closing their pages to the advertisements of patent medicines; legislation was appearing in several states; the public had been awakened to the fraud practised upon it, and a Federal Pure Food and Drug Act was beginning to be talked about." By 1920, Bok could write: "The pages of every newspaper and periodical of recognized standing are closed to the advertisements of patent medicines."

What Bok did was to mesh the editorial and advertising policies of his magazine—a merger resisted by most contemporary publishers who, I think, are often overzealous in their participation in community affairs and not zealous enough when it comes to controlling what appears in their advertising columns.

There have been occasional exceptions. In 1981, for instance, the *Chicago Sun Times* exposed abuses and profiteering in abortion clinics. Just before the series ran, at the suggestion of the reporter who wrote the series, the newspaper canceled advertising contracts, which were worth $600,000 a year, with the clinics.

Because the issue has been debated for so long, the acceptance of cigarette advertising offers a test of how journalists view their responsibility. The two sides have been clearly expressed by Michael Gartner, former president of the Des Moines Register and Tribune Company, and Sam Zagoria, the former ombudsman of the *Washington Post*.

In 1984, as a member of the Twentieth Century Fund Task Force on the Communication of Scientific Risk, Gartner commented:

> The public has been informed about the perils of smoking; it has, in large part, decided to keep smoking. The press did its job, the public did its. It is not the function of the press to keep beating people over the head to quit smoking. The press is not your mother.

The following year, after the AMA proposed its advertising ban, Zagoria took a more expansive and humanistic view of press responsibility:

> Hardly a day goes by without an editorial or columnist in some newspaper spanking a corporation or an industry for coming up short on social responsibility. Frequent visitors to the editorial knee, for example, have been the chemical companies for dumping cancer-producing waste.
>
> In this era of voluntarism, when the business community is constantly urging Congress and regulatory agencies to stand aside and "let us take care of the problem ourselves," couldn't the newspapers of the country agree–voluntarily and collectively–to refuse cigarette advertising? Couldn't they do what is right rather than only what is not prohibited by law?

Most papers take great pride in the service they render to their communities, not only in providing information but also in philanthropic activities that provide scholarships and underwrite athletic tournaments. Is not helping some youngster avert the tortures of life-shortening lung cancer even a greater gift? A greater service?

Publishers need not synchronize their advertising and editorial policies. But there are special circumstances—like advertisements for patent medicines at the turn of the century, like advertisements for abortion clinics in Chicago, and like advertisements for cigarettes—where publishers can apply to their advertising columns some of the same zeal they reserve for their editorial pages, thereby enhancing their credibility and proving they are socially responsible.

2 / The Legal Landscape

*The beleaguered tobacco companies. . .do have the right,
given the First Amendment, to present their case and extol
their products through advertising.*

—Editorial, *The Stamford Advocate*, December 27, 1985

*There ought not to be a law—there must never be a law—
against advertising anything society decides is legal.*

—Editorial, *USA Today*, December 19, 1985

• Early in 1985, Paula Hawkins (R.-Florida) held hearings to
determine whether Congress ought to pass a law barring beer
and wine advertising from radio and television, as was done fifteen years earlier with cigarettes. The supporters of such legislation claimed that advertisements glamorize alcohol and contribute to drunk driving fatalities and health problems arising
from drinking.

• In the spring of 1985, Representative John Sieberling (R.-
Ohio) introduced the fairness-in-alcohol advertising bill, which
would require that when beer or wine is advertised on television, radio, or cable, equivalent time be provided for a message
on the harmful effects of alcohol.

• At the end of 1985, the AMA proposed a ban on the promotion and marketing of cigarettes, claiming that "a government
prohibition of tobacco advertising would not strike at the core
of the First Amendment, which was designed to establish the
editorial freedom of the press and the right to religious, political,
artistic and scientific expression." In June 1986, the AMA proposal was introduced as formal legislation, and two congressional hearings on it were held during the summer.

Although unlikely to be enacted into law, these proposals raise a host of legal and ethical issues involving interpretations of the First Amendment, the application of the Fairness Doctrine, and the existence—or lack thereof—of a "right to advertise."

"Commercial Speech" and the First Amendment

Despite the absolute language of the First Amendment— Congress shall make "no law" restricting freedom of speech or the press—constitutional protection is not afforded to all classes of speech. Over the past fifteen years, the Supreme Court has afforded substantial—but not total—protection to "commercial speech."* The Court has said that commercial speech deserves protection because "it not only serves the economic interest of the speaker, but also assists consumers and furthers societal interest in the fullest dissemination of information." But the Court has also noted that the government may ban commercial speech that is deceptive or related to illegal activity and may restrict it when there is a substantial governmental interest in doing so. It is the last point that those advocating advertising bans argue from. They claim that preventing smoking and alcohol-related deaths qualifies as "a substantial state interest."

The issues involved in the arguments over commercial speech are complicated by the different treatment given print and electronic media in this nation. The electronic media have never been given the same degree of constitutional freedom as the print media—and so it does not follow that just because cigarette advertising was banned from television that it can be banned from print. Nor does it necessarily follow that just because cigarette advertising was banned from television, a ban on beer and wine advertising can pass constitutional muster. (The makers of distilled sprits have decided voluntarily not to advertise.) In a letter to Senator Hawkins in 1985, however, Marc A. Franklin of Stanford Law School, a leading authority on the First Amendment, predicted that a properly drafted statute banning beer and wine advertising would be upheld by the Supreme Court on the ground that "public safety concerns are offered as

---

*In July 1986, in a puzzling case, the Supreme Court seemed to retreat from its position of giving commercial speech greater freedom. In a 5-4 decision, the Court said Puerto Rico could forbid the casinos it licenses from using local advertising to solicit gamblers on the island.

primary justifications for the limits on what would otherwise be protected speech."

There is almost no case law on whether legislation that bans a harmful substance from being advertised in newspapers or magazines is constitutional (the Utah Supreme Court, fifteen years ago, struck down as unconstitutional a state law banning newspaper advertising of cigarettes). Once the rhetorical underbrush is cleared away, several important signposts suggest that the constitutionality of such a proposal is in doubt. What we know now is:

- Congress has required a health warning on labels of cigarettes.
- Congress has banned cigarette advertising on radio and television, a ban that was upheld by the Supreme Court.
- This legislation applies to television because the airwaves are public and because broadcasting is an intrusive medium that presumably inordinately influences minors—and the sale of cigarettes is generally forbidden to minors.*
- Since the mid-1970s, the Supreme Court has made it plain that while it considers commercial speech worthy of certain First Amendment protections, such speech does not stand on a par with the kind of political speech that lies at the core of the First Amendment. The precise limits of the protection of commercial speech are still being refined.
- In 1980, in *Central Hudson Gas and Electric Corp. v. Public Services Commission*, the Supreme Court struck down a state restriction on advertising that appears to be narrower than the complete ban on tobacco product advertising being proposed by the AMA. (Since then, several lower federal courts have sustained state liquor advertising bans, based in part on the Twenty-First Amendment, which repealed Prohibition and grants states special authority to regulate alcohol.)

---

*As a practical matter, this ban may be peculiar to a period of extraordinary activism by the Federal Communications Commission (FCC), during which the Fairness Doctrine was interpreted to apply to product advertising. That doctrine requires television and radio to deal with controversial issues and to present contrasting viewpoints on them. The doctrine no longer applies to such commercials. And it has never applied to print, which means that the government cannot compel a newspaper, as it did television, to air free advertisements questioning a product whose manufacturers paid large sums of money to have promoted.

In discussing possible legislation and its constitutionality, it is critical to remember that laws do not operate in a vacuum of statutes and cases. They are anchored in the empirical world. Whether a legislative ban on the advertising of a hazardous product is appropriate depends in part on two factors: how dangerous the product is to the user's health and whether advertising enlarges its market. The arguments used to restrict cigarette advertising and alcohol advertising are similar, and presumably would apply in the future to other hazardous products.

The Media View of the Law

About the only legal certainty is that newspapers and magazines are not obligated by the First Amendment, by the laws of unfair competition, or by any other laws to carry advertising that they do not wish to publish. No court has yet forced a newspaper or magazine to accept an advertisement. The articles, editorials, and columns that appeared following the AMA proposal showed little awareness of the complicated and unsettled state of the other legal questions yet to be answered and the legal subtleties involved in answering them.

Carl Rowan, a *Washington Post* columnist, decried the AMA proposal: "In a free society, any product that is legal ought to be advertisable, promotable. I think it was a First Amendment outrage that in 1971 Congress outlawed tobacco ads on radio and television." Some editorials misstated the law. For example, on December 12, 1985, the *St. Petersburg Times* said:

> To state the obvious, this newspaper accepts cigarette advertising. The loss of that revenue would be felt, though we could learn to live without it. We wish, in fact, that nobody smoked. *But so long as tobacco is a legal product, we don't have the right to refuse that advertising.* Nor does Congress have the right to ban it. [Emphasis added.]

Many reporters and commentators accepted, without question, positions presented by advocates. They treated as fact mere assumptions that needed to be tested. There was little or no analysis of whether the positions of the AMA, its allies, or its opponents were accurate reflections of the law. And it should come as no surprise that greater weight was given to the arguments of the tobacco industry and media spokesmen—in part because reporters and editors react almost reflexively when they hear the words "First Amendment."

The position of the Tobacco Institute, the Washington-based industry trade group, succinctly, but simplistically, stated the anti-AMA position: "Cigarettes are a legal product. The right to truthfully advertise legal products without government interference has been upheld by the Supreme Court." This position was echoed by trade groups representing newspaper and magazine publishers. In a letter, Jerry W. Friedheim, executive vice president of the American Newspaper Publishers Association, and William Gorog, president of the Magazine Publishers Association, appealed to the AMA not to vote for a cigarette ban, saying:

> We take no position here with respect to health risks. Our concern is that any such risks not be misused in an unconstitutional attempt to restrict free speech in a free society.
>
> Products that can be legally sold in our society are entitled to be advertised; if it is legal to sell a product, it should be legal to advertise it. This "commercial speech" is Constitutionally protected.

But there is no such thing as a constitutionally guaranteed "right to advertise," just as there is no constitutionally guaranteed consumers' "right to know." Neither of these "rights" carries the legal power to compel others to dispense information to the public at large. Publishers decide what goes in their publications. They cannot be compelled to accept advertising, just as they cannot be compelled to run a news story.

Moreover, it is by no means certain that anyone is *entitled* to advertise, as the Friedheim-Gorog letter states. In fact, in the few cases that deal with this issue, courts have said just the opposite. For instance, in a 1971 case, *Chicago Joint Board, Amalgamated Clothing Workers v. Chicago Tribune Co.*, a union tried to place an advertisement urging the reduction in the importation of foreign clothing. All four Chicago newspapers relied on the Marshall Field department store for substantial advertising revenues, and two of these papers were owned by Field Enterprises, also the parent company of the big department store. All of them turned down the union advertisement. A district court dismissed the union's lawsuit on the grounds that a newspaper is a private enterprise and has an absolute right to reject advertising with or without telling anyone why. The dismissal of the case was sustained on appeal. This case, said Benno C. Schmidt, Jr., in 1976 in *Freedom of the Press v. Public Access*, "presents a positive conception of constitutional interest in preserving the privacy of the press from obligatory publication."

Cigarette Advertising on Television: A Case Study

The richly intricate legislative history of the ban on cigarette advertising provides a key to whether advertising bans of cigarettes in print, of alcohol on television, or of other products in either media can constitutionally be enacted.

The current debate on cigarette advertising has its roots in 1964 when Dr. Luther L. Terry, the surgeon general, reported that "cigarette smoking contributes substantially to mortality." The surgeon general's report was quickly followed by regulations aimed at curbing smoking. In 1965, Congress enacted legislation requiring a health warning to be placed on all cigarette packages.

In 1967, the FCC applied the Fairness Doctrine to the advertising of cigarettes on the air, ruling that broadcasters had to "donate" air time—not equal time or even equally effective time, but significant air time—to the American Cancer Society and other organizations to rebut cigarette commercials and to point out that smoking "may be hazardous to the smoker's health." In practice, it worked out that one anti-smoking commercial was permitted for every three or four smoking advertisements. The FCC ruling was the result of efforts by John F. Banzhaf III, then a young New York lawyer who now heads Action on Smoking and Health (ASH), a Washington-based anti-smoking organization. The next year, 1968, the United States Court of Appeals for the District of Columbia upheld the FCC determination.

As Thomas Whiteside wrote in *The New Yorker* in 1970, the result of the FCC ruling was that the television audience was exposed to a number of "anti-smoking messages, which seemed to have the capacity of acting upon the existing crowd of cigarette commercials like antibodies grappling with some bacterial swarm." More recently, Ron M. Landsman, a lawyer in Washington, D.C. specializing in health-care issues, offered a similarly graphic simile: "Like a coyote that chews off its leg to escape from a trap, the industry wanted to cut out all broadcast advertising to stop the flow of anti-smoking ads."

What happened, according to several surveys, was that the anti-smoking messages had a significant impact in lowering consumption of cigarettes. The tobacco companies did not wish to stop advertising for fear of losing their competitive position; yet every commercial they bought to advance their product triggered the airing of more anti-smoking advertisements. The more money they spent, the more anti-smoking commercials were aired, and the more customers they lost.

The tobacco manufacturers were facing additional pressures. In February 1969, the FCC had issued a public notice that it intended to propose a ruling to ban cigarette advertising from television and radio altogether. The previous year, the Federal Trade Commission (FTC) had made it known that it wished to require stronger health warnings on cigarette packs.

The first cigarette labeling act, enacted in 1965, contained a critical preemption clause that prohibited the FCC and other regulatory agencies from taking action against tobacco advertising on the grounds of health. This was scheduled to expire in 1969, and manufacturers were afraid that if the preemption clause did lapse, a number of bills then pending in state legislatures would be enacted. These bills would have restricted tobacco sales and advertising.

Rather than oppose the banning of cigarette advertising, broadcasters and, to a larger extent, the manufacturers, acquiesced. Broadcasters feared that the advertising of products other than cigarettes might be regulated and subject to the Fairness Doctrine. Manufacturers were concerned about the success of the anti-smoking messages. Each, it turned out, had something to gain from restrictive legislation.

In his useful chronology in *The New Yorker*, Whiteside noted, "Under pressure from the Senate, and out of fear that if federal regulatory agencies stepped in to do something about cigarette advertising on the air a great deal of advertising might suffer the same fate, the broadcasters gave in, and in July 1969 announced a plan to phase out all kinds of cigarette advertising over a three-and-a-half-year period beginning January 1, 1970.

In what initially appeared to be an act of great corporate responsibility, Joseph Cullman III, chairman of Philip Morris, Inc., promised on behalf of the nine leading cigarette manufacturers to end all cigarette advertising on radio and television. Cullman stressed what he felt were the unique qualities of television in testimony before Congress in July 1969: "I think further that broadcast is quite different from print media. We think that the print media appeals to a more adult person and as such is a more appropriate place for cigarette ads."

Congress subsequently enacted the Public Health Cigarette Smoking Act of 1969, which provided that after January 1, 1971, "It shall be unlawful to advertise cigarettes on any medium of electronic communication subject to the jurisdiction of the Federal Communications Commission." The Public Health Cigarette Smoking Act was signed into law by President Nixon on April 1, 1970, and took effect nine months later, at the end

of New Year's Day, right after the final college football games of
the season, allowing the networks to reap a last windfall of tobacco revenues.

Although they suffered a short-term loss of revenues, in the
long run broadcasters got what they wanted. In 1974, the commission repudiated its cigarette ruling and adopted a policy of
applying the Fairness Doctrine only to those commercials that
"are devoted in an obvious and meaningful way to the discussion of public issues," which exempted advertising from the
Fairness Doctrine.

The Pandora's box opened by Banzhaf's victory was closed.
That victory prompted a wave of demands for counter-commer-
cials to answer advertisements for leaded gasoline, snowmobiles,
trash compactors, and other products felt to be hazardous to consumers. One New York resident, representing a group called
"Children Before Dogs," petitioned for counter-advertisements
balancing dog food commercials that, he claimed, encouraged
pet ownership without addressing the concerns that pets led to
disease and excessive sewage in New York City streets. In its ruling, in 1972, the commission said that dog food commercials
did not raise a matter of important public controversy, and the
FCC's 1974 action put the controversy to a rest, at least for a
decade.

Tobacco manufacturers got what they wanted from the legislation: The anti-smoking forces no longer received free air time.
Only those anti-smoking groups who could afford to buy time
remained on the air. Moreover, the manufacturers were able to
circumvent the ban in part by sponsoring sports and cultural
events, where their names and logos have been prominently
displayed. And Congress stiffened warnings but forbade stricter
state regulation of cigarette advertising and packaging.*

In *Capital Broadcasting Co. v. Mitchell*, a federal court in 1971
upheld the ban of cigarette advertising on television.

The plaintiffs complained that the attempt by Congress to
classify media into two categories—those prohibited from carrying cigarette advertisements and those who are not—con-

---

*Even though they clearly state the dangers of smoking, there is not much
empirical evidence that these federally mandated warnings have deterred people from smoking. What the law requiring the package warnings has done
so far is protect the manufacturers from product-liability suits. They have
asserted successfully that their customers had been warned of the dangers.
Early in 1986, a federal appeals court in Philadelphia held that federally mandated health warnings protect the industry from claims that it failed to warn

travenes the Fifth Amendment because the distinctions drawn are "arbitrary and invidious."

The majority ruled that Congress had been justified in distinguishing television from print, largely because of television's impact on children. The court looked to the legislative intent in the passage of the 1969 law:

> Thus, Congress knew of the close relationship between cigarette commercials broadcast on the electronic media and their potential influence on young people, and was no doubt aware that the younger the individual the greater the reliance on the broadcast message rather than the written word. A pre-school or early elementary school age child can hear and understand a radio commercial or see, hear and understand a television commercial, while at the same time be substantially unaffected by an advertisement printed in a newspaper, magazine or appearing on a billboard.

The court found that Congress could "rationally distinguish" television and radio from other media because the public owns the airwaves and because licensees "must operate broadcast facilities in the public interest under the supervision of a federal regulatory agency."

In a dissent, J. Skelly Wright condemned cigarettes:

> Overwhelming scientific evidence makes plain that the Salem girl was in fact a seductive merchant of death—that the real Marlboro Country is the graveyard.

But he objected to the banning of advertising because "the theory of free speech is grounded on the belief that people will make the right choice if presented with all points of view on a controversial issue." It is likely that the rationale of this dissent—

---

consumers adequately that cigarettes are dangerous or that its advertising has the effect of negating the warning.

The reporting on this significant decision was, with few exceptions, another dreadful example of the shallow reporting on much of this issue. Most papers missed the story, and once they caught up, they reported it as a lopsided victory for tobacco interests. It was a victory for them, but it was only one federal appeals court speaking. The issue may eventually be resolved by the Supreme Court. While it was a major setback for anti-smoking advocates, it was not a knockout. Many reporters found out about the decision a day after it was handed down at a press conference arranged by a public relations firm for a tobacco company. In some stories, financial reporters authoritatively quoted securities analysts—who possessed no discernible legal credentials— about the legal consequences of the case. The analysts were offering mere speculation.

written before the Supreme Court afforded protection to commercial speech—would form the basis of a successful attack on
any attempt to regulate cigarette advertising today.

The opinion was affirmed without an opinion by the Supreme
Court in 1972. It is the only reported Supreme Court case dealing with cigarette advertising and one of a handful dealing with
advertising prohibitions. But since it predated decisions protecting commercial speech, its precedential value, even as it
relates to television and radio, is uncertain.

The Supreme Court Protects "Commercial Speech"

In a series of cases beginning in the mid-1970s, the Supreme
Court granted some degree of constitutional protection to
commercial speech. The Court's present posture on freedom of
speech in advertising was defined most clearly in 1980 in *Central Hudson*. That case involved a New York State regulation prohibiting utility advertisements from promoting the use of elec-
tricity on the ground that such advertising was contrary to the
national policy of conserving energy.

The Court held the government interest in conserving energy,
while important, could not overcome the utility's right to free
speech. Writing for the majority, Lewis F. Powell, Jr., said:

> Commercial expression not only serves the economic interest of the speaker,
> but also assists consumers and furthers the societal interest in the fullest
> possible dissemination of information. In applying the First Amendment
> to this area, we have rejected the "highly pluralistic" view that government
> has complete power to suppress or regulate commercial speech.

In a concurring opinion, Harry Blackmun, joined by William
Brennan, said it appeared that the majority would permit the
state to bar all direct advertising of air conditioning. "If a governmental unit believes that use or overuse of air conditioning is
a serious problem," he wrote, "it must attack that problem directly, by prohibiting air conditioning or regulating thermostat
levels." Furthermore, he wrote:

> I seriously doubt whether suppression of information concerning the
> availability and price of a legally offered product is ever a permissible way
> for the State to "dampen" demand for or use of the product.... No dif-
> ferences between commercial speech and other protected speech justify
> suppression of commercial speech in order to influence public conduct
> through manipulation of the availability of information.

This concurrence, of course, carries no weight as precedent; but its reasoning could be influential if ever a ban on print cigarette advertising were to be tested in court.

The majority said that the government could regulate advertisements for products only if the following four-part test were met:

1. At the outset, it must be determined whether the expression is protected by the First Amendment. It must concern a lawful activity and not be misleading.

2. The statute furthers a "substantial interest" of society.

3. The statute directly advances the essential governmental interest.

4. The benefits of the statute cannot be achieved by less restrictive measures.

This same four-part test was employed by the Court in July 1986 in upholding Puerto Rico's tight restriction on local advertising of casino gambling. In the majority opinion, William Rehnquist wrote that if a government can prohibit gambling entirely, as most states do, "it is permissible for the government to take the less intrusive step" of allowing gambling "but reducing the demand through restrictions on advertising."

In one ambiguous part of the opinion, Rehnquist noted that "legislative regulation of products or activities deemed harmful, such as cigarettes, alcoholic beverages, and prostitution, has varied from outright prohibition on the one hand. . .to legalization of the product or activity with restrictions on stimulation of its demand on the other." He continued: "To rule out the latter, intermediate kind of response would require more than we find in the First Amendment."

It is not clear what Rehnquist was getting at. For instance, he merely could have been referring to the fact that cigarette advertising has been banned on television; and, in a footnote, he cited the ban of cigarette advertising on television. Yet, many publications seemed to draw conclusions not warranted by the justice's words. Without even mentioning that the Court upheld the ban on casino advertising, the *Washington Post*, in its front-page headline, said: "Court Seems to Allow Banning of Cigarette and Alcohol Ads." With no substantiation, *Editor & Publisher*, the trade weekly, suggested the opinion would "clear the legal obstacles to the proposed ban on tobacco and alcohol advertising."

Later, *Editor & Publisher* editorialized: "It won't take the anti-liquor and anti-tobacco forces long to marshal their forces to take advantage of the precedent just set by the court."

In the opinion, *Posados de Puerto Rico v. Tourism Company,* the Court relied heavily on *Central Hudson,* which, until modified, remains the key precedent relating to commercial speech.

In *Central Hudson,* the Court found that the speech was protected by the First Amendment and that the claimed government interest in energy conservation was substantial. However, since the state did not satisfactorily demonstrate a direct relationship between advertising prohibition and the legislative objectives, or that a more limited restriction would not adequately serve these interests, the law was held unconstitutional.

By analogy, in order for a hypothetical statute banning print cigarette advertising to pass constitutional muster, the following would need to be shown:

- *The speech is protected by the First Amendment* because it does not relate to unlawful activity and is not misleading.
- *Smoking poses a threat to health,* which is a "substantial interest" of society.
- *Tobacco advertising is a critical reason that people smoke.* This provides the necessary link to demonstrate that the hypothetical statute advances the societal interest of having people stop smoking.
- *Less restrictive alternatives are not available* to induce people to stop smoking.

The Speech is Protected by the First Amendment
For the sake of the hypothetical, we can assume the advertising is concerned with a lawful product, cigarettes, and is not misleading—that is, it does not say that "smoking Brand X guarantees good grades." Therefore, it meets the first criterion.

Does Smoking Pose a Threat to Health?
Some serious scholars believe that the case against smoking is unproven and that much remains to be explored. For example, *Smoking and Society,* an anthology published in 1986 by Lexington Books, contains several essays questioning the statistical and scientific credibility of the widely held view that smoking causes health problems.

These doubts are reinforced by the tobacco companies. "What we're saying is that there are a lot of unanswered questions out there," Betsy Anness, manager of external communications for R. J. Reynolds Tobacco Co., said in an interview with the *Chicago Tribune*. She was defending controversial advertisements which said: "Studies that conclude that smoking causes disease have regularly ignored significant evidence to the contrary." Her defense was that "it has never been proven conclusively that cigarette smoking is the cause of any disease in humans."*

But most medical research suggests an overwhelming case against smoking. On "Face the Nation" in December 1985, C. Everett Koop, the surgeon general, said:

> I can tell you absolutely that since 1964 there have been in excess of 50,000 scientific articles in reputable journals that have taken the opposite point of view of R. J. Reynolds. If you sell cigarettes, what can you do in the face of scientific evidence except to say it's not right.

Dr. William Bennett, writing in the March 1985 issue of the *Harvard Medical School Health Letter*, said:

> Contrary to the impression sometimes given by the manufacturers, what serious scientific controversy there ever was about the ill effects of cigarette smoking has long since been settled. There are still some areas of uncertainty, but the main point is rock-solid: as a group, cigarette smokers die earlier than nonsmokers.

A conclusive correlation between smoking and age of death is arguably sufficient to establish a substantial state interest in banning tobacco advertising. (It is less certain whether the consumption of beer and wine poses such a health risk. So far, no link has been shown between the moderate consumption of beer and wine and adverse health effects. Clearly, there is a legitimate state interest in restricting the *abuse* of alcohol, such as driving under the influence. But, while cigarettes are considered to be inherently harmful, a growing body of medical evidence suggests that moderate drinkers may have reduced the risks for the development of heart disease.)

Is Tobacco Advertising a Critical Reason that People Smoke? "The evidence isn't all that clear," says Barry Lynn, the

---

*In June 1986, the FTC charged in a complaint that an R. J. Reynolds advertisement was "false or misleading" because it understated the risks of smoking. In August 1986, an administrative law judge ruled that the complaint should be dismissed because the First Amendment fully protected such an "editorial advertisement."

legislative counsel of the American Civil Liberties Union, "that people begin to smoke because they see a dancing cigarette pack or a Kool ad on the subway."

In a legal memorandum prepared for the Tobacco Institute in response to the AMA proposal, the Washington law firm of Covington & Burling stated with clarity the position of the industry toward advertising:

> The sole purpose and clear effect of tobacco product advertising is to enhance brand competition—that is, to reinforce existing brand preferences and/or to create new ones among persons who already use such products.

The same arguments of brand preferences are made by beer and wine manufacturers, who say that advertising affects only market share rather than overall consumption. This is the way that Les Brown, editor-in-chief of *Channels* magazine, reacted to that argument:

> You have to be some kind of simp to believe that large corporations, spending millions of dollars through agencies that are masters of persuasion, aren't trying to sell a whole new generation on the pleasures of drink while planting the seeds of brand loyalty.

Philip Dougherty, the respected advertising columnist for *The New York Times*, took a similarly jaundiced view of the limited claims that are made by the advertising industry. In a column he wrote after the AMA announced its proposal, Dougherty first noted that the "reaction in adland" was "an almost universal condemnation based on First Amendment rights." Then Dougherty wryly observed that despite the hundreds of millions of dollars spent annually on cigarette advertising, "the advertising industry stoutly insists that cigarette advertising does not get people to start smoking." Further, he said, "there have been enough top advertising executives doing guest shots on TV news shows related to the AMA declaration in the last couple of days—all but saying that advertising does not work—to put the business back a decade."

One report, prepared by the Bureau of Economics of the FTC, said that most of the studies of cigarette company advertising have found that changes in total advertising have little or no effect on total consumption. But the report, which discusses the potential effects of a ban on alcoholic beverages advertising, pointed out that most of these studies dealt with relatively small variations in the amount of advertising. "It would not follow," the report concluded, "that banning all advertising, or all broadcast advertising, would have little or no effect."

When looking for guidance to countries where cigarette advertising has been banned, advocates of either side of the controversy have found ammunition to support their position. "If I had my way, I would certainly ban advertising," said the surgeon general after the AMA proposal was announced. "The experience in countries where advertising bans have been enforced has shown a tremendous drop in smoking."* But a study conducted for the International Advertising Association concluded: "There is no evidence from those countries where tobacco advertising has been banned that the ban has been accompanied by a significant reduction in overall consumption, per capita consumption or incidence of smoking."

Probably more important than any of these reports is what the Supreme Court itself said in the *Central Hudson* case. The Court found "an immediate connection" between advertising and energy consumption, noting that the utility would not have contested the advertising ban unless it believed that advertising would increase its sales. Since *Central Hudson*, two federal appeals courts, in upholding state legislative bans of liquor advertising, have also acknowledged that it is reasonable to link advertising to consumption. One appeals court wrote:

> It is beyond our ability to understand why huge sums of money would be devoted to the promotion of sales of liquor without expected results. . . .We simply do not believe that the liquor industry spends a billion dollars a year on advertising solely to acquire an added market share at the expense of competitors.

While *Central Hudson* did find the contested New York law unconstitutional, it did not definitively strike down "bans on advertising that are not misleading or deceptive or related to unlawful activity." This is shown in the string of cases involving the advertising of liquor, a product legal in most places—

---

*In August 1986, Koop testified that he favored a bill sponsored by Representative Mike Synar, an Alabama Democrat, that would ban the advertising and promoting of tobacco products. Taking a position contrary to the Reagan administration, Koop said that tobacco promotion "increases the total universe of users and increases consumption by those who already use it." Advertising, he said, attracts new smokers, makes lapsed smokers resume smoking, increases consumption by providing external cues for smokers, and makes it harder for smokers to quit.

but subject to special consideration under the Twenty-First Amendment, which is unique in the constitutional scheme in that it grants states special authority to regulate alcohol.

In 1983, for example, the Fifth Circuit Court of Appeals upheld Mississippi's ban on liquor advertising, saying that the harmful effects of alcohol consumption more than outweigh any First Amendment considerations. The court said:

> If there is any instance where a state can escape First Amendment constraint while prohibiting truthful advertising promoting lawful sales, it would be where the product being sold is intoxicating liquor.

Such cases seem to have been generally overlooked by press commentators on the AMA proposal, many of whom concluded that, without exception, the First Amendment prohibits any government restraints on lawful advertising.

Are Less Restrictive Alternatives Available?

There are several ways to regulate cigarette and alcohol consumption that *conceivably* would be less restrictive than an advertising ban:

• Require mandatory counteradvertisements. This would mean the Fairness Doctrine would be reinterpreted to apply to products (and the broadcast ban against cigarettes repealed). Given the difficulty the FCC had in the early 1970s in limiting the scope of the doctrine, this approach seems unlikely.

• Restrict beer and wine advertising on television to certain late night hours when children are less likely to watch. Similarly, in newspapers and magazines, cigarette advertisements could be restricted to advertisements known as tombstone advertisements that contain just text.

Tombstone advertisements would eliminate many of the misgivings about advertising that the FTC expressed to Congress in its report on cigarette advertising in the summer of 1985. The FTC noted that:

> Cigarette manufacturers continued to concentrate on associating smoking with success and a luxurious lifestyle. Ads were designed to imply a relationship between smoking and healthy living by using sports and outdoor activities. Often cigarette ads were set in scenic areas where smiling, happy people were engaged in various outdoor activities.

The report added that cigarette advertising "also strived to present a positive image of the cigarette smoker, who was most frequently posed against various backgrounds connoting pleasure and enjoyment. The luxury smoking themes were juxtaposed with depictions of success and delivered a message that smoking was the way to go to reach high goals."

In March 1986, the American Cancer Society, "as a first step," called for the elimination of all models and scenery in cigarette advertising, recommending that "advertising copy should merely feature the tar and nicotine content of the product, one of the four rotating warning messages from the Surgeon General, and the price of the product."

• Support counterspeech. In rejecting the AMA proposal for an advertising ban, *Advertising Age* editorialized:

> Put together an advertising fund, AMA. . . . Hire an ad agency. . . . If cigarette ads depict smoking as glamorous, show its unglamorous aspects. If a cigarette ad shows an attractive, athletic young woman, run an ad showing a haggard, harried middle-aged woman puffing away. If a cigarette ad shows a high-flying snowmobile and relates that image to its brand, then show an emphysema patient with an oxygen tank strapped to the wheelchair. Use your patients as your role models. Or enlist the aid of celebrities who've kicked the habit; have them talk about it. Use sports figures to talk about the detrimental ways tobacco affects the body. . . .

Similar suggestions have been made to run advertisements to counter alcohol abuse. This is all well and good, but in order for counterspeech to be effective, those attacking the advertising must have resources roughly equivalent to the advertisers or some sort of mechanism must compel the publication or broadcast stations to run these advertisements. At present, the resources of the cigarette makers and beer and wine manufacturers are unmatched by those of their critics.

The Fairness Doctrine, of course, does not apply to print, and newspapers may refuse such advertisements. In a 1982 case, *Diamond v. World News Corp.*, Morris Lasker, a federal judge in Manhattan, ruled that a newspaper may unilaterally refuse to run an anti-smoking advertisement without violating the antitrust laws—so long as there is no evidence of conspiracy between the newspaper and its cigarette advertisers.

• Tax advertising. A collateral attack specifically dealing with cigarette advertising has been proposed by Senator Bill Bradley, the New Jersey Democrat, and Representative Fortney H. "Pete" Stark, a California Democrat. Early in 1986, Bradley introduced legislation that would disallow tax deductions for the cost of advertising and promoting tobacco products:

on public health campaigns to warn people of the
_.co. At the same time we allow tobacco manufacturers to
_.11ons of dollars in advertising expenses that are aimed at en-
_.ing people to smoke.

If this legislation is enacted and companies continue to advertise, they would have to pay more taxes. This would lead to
higher prices, and "hopefully," says Stark, to lower consumption:

> If the companies choose to stop promotional activities, then we will have
> achieved the beneficial effect of a ban without the potential constitutional
> problems associated with an outright ban.

A memorandum prepared by the American Law Division of the
Congressional Research Service of the Library of Congress concluded that "the proposed legislation would likely pass constitutional muster."

Arrayed against this legislation are the same people oppos-
ing the more far-reaching AMA ban. The Tobacco Institute called
the Bradley-Stark proposal "censorship through taxation." Barry
Lynn of the American Civil Liberties Union said that the proposal was discriminatory because it is "content based." *Editor
& Publisher* editorialized: "This is not a 'revenue bill' but an
unconstitutional attempt to restrict truthful advertising of a product legally manufactured and sold." Such legislation, the trade
publication said, would be "a negation of the role advertising
has played in developing and maintaining our high standard of
living."

This legislation probably has a better chance than the AMA
proposal, which was finally introduced as legislation six months
after it was initially proposed. Kirk Johnson, AMA's general
counsel, thinks that if enacted the total ban would stand up
because tobacco's damage to health is well documented and there
is evidence that advertising increases its consumption—
positions sharply contested by the tobacco industry.

At this point, though, such a prohibition appears to run
counter to most recent Supreme Court cases affording constitutional protection to commercial speech. Floyd Abrams, a leading
First Amendment lawyer who has represented newspapers and
networks and who on occasion has advised tobacco companies,
concludes: "A flat ban on the sale of a product that is lawful
to buy and sell is likely unconstitutional.... In short, if you can
sell a product, why can't you advertise it?"

The answer probably is: You can advertise it, but you do not
have to do so.

3 / The Question of Acceptability

The Daily Record *established a policy of refusing cigarette advertising about 15 years ago. . . .Unfortunately, some of the nation's major publications have failed to follow suit; however, the freedom to be selective in the advertising they accept is, and should remain, their prerogative.*

—Editorial, Morristown (New Jersey) *Daily Record,*
December 13, 1985

"The power of a privately owned newspaper to advance its own political, social and economic views is bounded by only two factors," the Supreme Court noted in a 1973 case, *Columbia Broadcasting System v. Democratic National Committee,* "first, the acceptance of a sufficient number of readers—and hence advertisers—to assure financial success; and second, the journalistic integrity of its editors and publishers."

The following year, in *Miami Herald Publishing Company v. Tornillo,* the Supreme Court said that a statute that enforced access for noncommercial "public issue" advertising was unconstitutional. A newspaper, the Court said, "is more than a passive receptacle or conduit for news, comment and advertising."

The message from these cases is clear: The government has no role in dictating the content of a publication. It is up to individual publishers to print what they think is in the public interest—or in *their* interest. They may turn down advertisements that are unsuited to their audience or that they do not like. The issue is not whether publishers are obligated by the First Amendment or by the laws of unfair competition to carry advertising they do not wish to publish; rather it is whether they choose voluntarily not to accept advertisements.

A couple of years ago, Peter J. Caruso, a Boston lawyer specializing in media matters, summed up the state of the law: "The basic court-tested rule is that a newspaper can refuse to publish any ad, as long as the decision is unilateral, does not violate anti-trust laws, is not part of a conspiracy, or does not breach a contractual obligation." He then offered this cynical advice to readers of *Editor & Publisher*:

> Usually, a well-intentioned, candid response on the reasons for refusal has been the basis of the lawsuit—and usually its strongest point. After the manager has reviewed the questioned ad and decides unilaterally to refuse to publish it, the proper reply to the customer is: "At this time, the paper chooses not to accept your ad." Please do not say anymore. Do not elaborate. Do not offer suggestions as to copy changes. . . . Anything and everything you say will only encourage his belief that the newspaper has an illegal motive and is putting him out of business.

Although few laws dictate what can and cannot be advertised, by no means do all advertisements for lawful products appear. Most publications have adopted advertising policies, and some advertisers voluntarily restrict their own advertising. One group that polices itself is distillers, who have agreed not to advertise on television. In addition, beer and wine makers have adopted codes that limit what they say in their advertisements. Among the "twenty commandments" of the Brewing Industry Advertising Guidelines are:

> Beer advertisements should neither suggest nor encourage overindulgence.
> Beer advertising should not portray sexual passion, promiscuity or any other amorous activity as a consequence of drinking beer.
> Beer advertising on television should make no representation of on-camera drinking, including sound effects of drinking.

Other restrictions affect advertisements of alcoholic beverages. For example, active professional athletes are prohibited from beer advertisements under a rule of the Bureau of Alcohol, Tobacco and Firearms, a division of the Treasury Department. The Wine Institute code stresses that wine is an accompaniment to food. One provision says: "Wine shall not be represented as vital to social responsibility or crucial for successful entertaining."

Media Advertising Codes

"We reserve the right to refuse any advertising which, in our opinion, is unacceptable," is the straightforward policy of *The Dallas Times Herald*. At *Newsweek*, advertising "that, in the publisher's opinion, offends large numbers of our subscribers, is fraudulent in content or approach, goes beyond generally accepted business practices or moral standards, or is just simply deemed inappropriate for *Newsweek*, is rejected."

Of the 110 publishers who responded to my questionnaire, about two-thirds reported they had written codes. Some, like the code adopted by the *Los Angeles Times*, are several hundred pages long; others are only a page or two.

The *Seattle Times* has no code. John A. Williams, vice president of sales and marketing for the paper, said:

> We mostly rely on common sense. This area is too complex to reduce all items to writing. Our basic philosophy is to allow access to everyone possible, allowing for legal constraints such as libel or slander, common decency and taste, or ads that are misleading or could harm the integrity of our product.

The almost universal response of publishers to my questionnaire was that they accept advertising for all lawful products. The *reality*, however, is different. Newspapers and magazines reject advertising for all sorts of reasons—some frivolous, others serious—and their policies generally reflect the values of their communities or audiences.

Moreover, advertising policies generally conform to a conventional view of the world. "Over the course of the years," recalled Thomas J. Masterson, advertising sales administration manager of *The Philadelphia Inquirer* and *Philadelphia Daily News*, "I've had to have prospective advertisers escorted from the premises; I was told 'I will see you in my place' by a gentleman who purported to be the Second Coming; I had a 'malocchio' (an evil-eye curse) not so gently placed upon my person by a gypsy woman who wanted to place an ad for her fortune telling establishment."

In 1980, the *San Bernadino Sun* said that it would no longer accept advertising for "the recruitment or aggrandizement" of the Ku Klux Klan. "We're putting our money where our mouth is—although it is not a lot of money," William Honeysett, publisher of the Gannett-owned newspaper, said at the time.

The two San Diego papers, the *Union* and *Evening Tribune,* do not accept advertisements from the Planned Parenthood Association or any birth control agencies or abortion clinics. In response to my questionnaire, ten publishers said that abortion advertisements created their greatest difficulties.

Some restrictions protect readers from seemingly innocent activities that are, in fact, illegal. For example, the *St. Petersburg Times* refuses advertisements offering for sale cats and dogs that are less than eight weeks old. No explanation is given. Such sales, it turns out, are prohibited under Florida law.

Other restrictions are designed to protect readers from ventures that seem harmful or possibly shady. Since 1985, *The Day* of New London, Connecticut, has not accepted advertisements for "Happy Hours" at bars, hoping that this measure will help to reduce the incidence of highway deaths. "It just seemed there was so much madness, we had to do something," said Reid McCluggage, publisher, president, and editor. "We are not in favor of censorship, but we are in favor of editing the newspaper, and that applies to advertising as well as news."

A number of papers are currently scrutinizing advertisements for work done at home—especially those that require respondents to pay out money. *The Columbus* (Nebraska) *Telegram* now refuses ads for "home sewing," while *The Sanford* (North Carolina) *Herald* casts a critical eye on "envelope stuffing."

Some advertising policies reflect the idiosyncracies of a community. *The Los Angeles Times,* for instance, has a special policy applying to smog. "Since few areas are not completely smog free," the policy states, "advertisers may not say 'no smog here,' 'smog free,' 'get out of the smog,' etc. They may use such phrases as 'where the air is cleaner,' 'cleaner skies in . . . ,' 'fresh desert air,' etc." The *Times* also declines advertisements for "streaking" services and any advertisements for wild animals.

In Boston, the temporary home to thousands of students, the *Globe* forbids "term paper agencies and other organizations or individuals offering to do academic work, papers, theses or research for others" from advertising their services. Nor, states the policy, "may they place 'Help Wanted' advertisements to hire others to perform similar work." The *Globe* is particularly indignant about such ventures: "We do NOT care to print these advertisements" is the phrasing of its policy.

Clearly then, many publications in the business of accepting advertising not only feel they have no obligation to accept all legal advertising, but they also feel it is their obligation to refuse these advertisements. The publishers whom I interviewed and surveyed often had difficulty articulating why they chose not to accept certain advertisements. Most often, though, they distinguished unacceptable advertisements on the basis of taste, morals, health, or religion.

Asked to identify his most troublesome problem in accepting advertising, Ric Trent, the publisher of *California* magazine, responded: "The plethora of cosmetic surgery clinics has created a huge number of visually disgusting ads. Trying to inject a standard of taste and still allow them access to the free market has been very difficult at times."

William James Mortimer, the publisher of the *Deseret News* in Salt Lake City, supported the AMA's call for a ban on cigarette advertising. His distaste for cigarettes is linked to the Mormon religion, which objects to smoking, and the advertising policy of the *Deseret News* reflects the stern religion in other ways:

> The *Deseret News*'s basic advertising policy is to accept non-deceptive, tasteful advertising of all lawful services, and all products that are legally manufactured and distributed, except the following:
> Liquor, beer, tobacco, tea and coffee, and X-rated motion pictures.
> Also, the *Deseret News* will not accept certain types of classified advertising pertaining to making contacts with marriage in mind, vasectomies, voluntary sterilization, and related subjects, and that do not meet the newspaper's criteria for morals.

The newspaper also bans classified advertisements for beauty contests.

Problems of advertising are often peculiar to an individual publication. A while ago, the *National Review* was swamped with advertisements offering such products as conservative bumper stickers and tie clips that were specifically designed for the conservative market. "At last," recalled William Rusher, the magazine's publisher, "the load of advertising became too heavy, in view of the requirement of editorial balance."

For a time, the magazine did not accept any advertisements of a "political nature," except for books. Its form rejection letter read: "We are struggling very hard to keep afloat, and must often make decisions of this painful kind for the benefit of both *National Review* and the conservative cause in general." The magazine eventually modified its policy and began accepting advertisements for bumper stickers and similar merchandise provided the advertisements were large. For Rusher, it was the "conservative cause" that prompted his action.

The advertising policy of the *Monterey* (California) *Peninsula Herald* is guided by its position as the only daily newspaper in its market area. "If we were to consistently align our advertising policy with our editorial policy, where does this leave the individual who wishes to espouse an opposite view?" asks Albert Cross, the paper's president and general manager. "For this reason," he added, "we tend to be generally quite liberal in our advertising acceptance standards so long as the matter submitted is not illegal, immoral, or patently and unfairly offensive to certain segments of our readership."

By far the most nettlesome problem for publishers is how to deal with advertisements with sexual content. In some ways, publications are more open than in the past. Popular features in many daily newspapers and magazines are the personal classified advertisements where people advertise to meet companions. These classifieds, which can be quite lucrative for publications, barely existed a few years ago. Although now considered generally acceptable, there still are limits: *New York Magazine*, for example, rejects personals seeking a one-night stand or a weekend rendezvous.

In other ways, publications reflect a very restricted and moralistic notion of what is permissible. In December 1978, *Playboy* magazine was preparing a feature on women in the Ivy League. At the time, the student newspapers were divided on whether to run a *Playboy* advertisement for women students willing to pose nude or seminude for the magazine.

Eight years later, in March 1986, the *Harvard Crimson* again refused to print a *Playboy* advertisement for recruiting sessions. Joseph S. Kahn, president of the *Crimson*, said: "After three hours of debate, we decided to reject the ad on the grounds that *Playboy* and the advertisement degrade women, and we at the *Crimson* did not want to aid the degradation by printing the ad." The *Playboy* advertisement ran in *The Boston Herald*, *The Boston Globe*, *The Boston Phoenix*, and in the *Harvard Independent*, a weekly publication. It also ran in other student publications in the Ivy League.

In the spring of 1986, under pressure from the media, the producers of a movie about two people who try to build a relationship out of a one-night stand changed the movie's title to "About last night...." The film was based on a prize-winning play by David Mamet titled "Sexual Perversity in Chicago," and that was the title that Tri-Star Pictures had originally chosen for the film. But there was opposition from television stations and newspapers. Stephen Randall, executive vice president-marketing for the movie company, said the reaction of some media was: "We won't take advertising with this title."

In the fall of 1985, David Lawrence, Jr., publisher of the *Detroit Free Press*, devoted a full column to a discussion of advertising of movies with sexual content. He set forth the criteria the paper employed in accepting such advertisements: Sexually suggestive copy and artwork will not be allowed, human bodies must be discreetly clad, and wording "will be reviewed for puns, double-meanings and the phraseology of the copy, including stage names." Finally, the policy said, "the sensitivities of our readers as well as other advertisers must be considered in determining the acceptability of all advertising." For example, before it ran the advertisement for the X-rated movie "Little Oral Annie," the paper changed the title to "Little Annie Takes Manhattan."

In conclusion, Lawrence attempted to reassure his audience of his concern for sexually explicit material: "We are part of the community, and the images we print and display can influence others. . . . I am troubled by 'trash.' But how free is a society where any individual or group of individuals determines what is 'trash' for everyone else?"

Earlier that year, Conrad A. Kloh, director of sales and marketing for *The Arizona Republic* and *The Phoenix Gazette*, carried on an extensive public correspondence with a reader over the appropriateness of accepting advertisements for "Peep's," an establishment featuring erotic dancers. Kloh defended the paper's decision to run them:

> Newspapers are in a perpetual quandary when it comes to the difficult problem of editing or rejecting advertising copy. As an enterprise protected by the First Amendment and jealous of the freedom that privilege gives us, we are very cautious in applying standards of publication (sometimes called censorship) to our advertisers, who we feel are entitled to that same freedom.
>
> In spite of that. . . there are some ads we will never take. We will not run, nor have we ever run, X-rated movies. *Bolero*, the latest Bo Derek epic, was turned down at a loss in revenue of at least $10,000. A stiff price to pay for a principle, no matter how large the company.
>
> We looked at the "Peep's" ad, as we do every advertisement we run, and accepted it because in our considered judgment it was within the bounds of current community standards for this day and age and directed to an adult audience where admission to minors was impossible.

As Kloh observed, principles can be costly. The *Cleveland Plain Dealer* refuses advertisements for escort services, for fortune tellers, and for handguns, except antiques. "We estimate over $500,000 a year is refused," said Alan Dant, advertising director of the paper.

The two extremes in the debate over advertising acceptability are not always profits and rectitude. Sometimes the decision to reject an advertisement becomes a straightforward cost-benefit analysis. The policy of New York's *Daily News*, for instance, is to "carefully examine" advertisements of competitors "to determine whether it is in keeping with the best interests of the *News*."

In 1984, the *Village Voice* turned down a full-page advertisement from a marginal competitor, *The Nation*. The advertisement, headlined, "Now Appearing Indefinitely in *The Nation* Magazine," listed eight *Nation* contributors in alphabetical order, including Alexander Cockburn, who had just been suspended from the *Voice* over a $10,000 grant he had accepted from an Arab studies organization. In the proposed advertisement, a cut-rate subscription coupon was included. A footnote read "Special offer to *Village Voice* readers: Subscribe to *The Nation* now, during Alexander Cockburn's 'indefinite suspension' from the *Voice*. If he is reinstated before your subscription ends, you may cancel, and we'll refund the remainder of your money on a pro rata basis."

John Evans, the *Voice* publisher, explained why the advertisement was rejected: "It's just not our policy to promote people who are directly competing with us in the marketplace. It's just not good business sense."

An item about the rejected advertisement, incidentally, was published in the *Voice*, a publication more open than most to self-criticism in its editorial columns.

Why "The Great Divide"

The most highly respected publishers deny that there is an ethical gulf between their ivory tower and their counting house. That position was articulated by Eugene Patterson, former editor and now chairman and chief executive officer of the *St. Petersburg Times*, in *Drawing the Line*, a book published in 1984 in which thirty-one editors describe their "toughest ethical dilemmas."

"Many readers," wrote Patterson, "see enough advertising accepted from sources we've denounced to assume revenue supersedes rectitude on our scale of values. They perceive money as our moral motivator. They do not turn around that assumption and give us credit for having the editorial valor to bite the hand that feeds us. I am convinced, even though I cannot convince our doubters, that our practice is the ethical one."

"There is a clear, well-defined line of separation between the news department of the *Tennessean* and the advertising department," said John Seigenthaler, who carries three titles— publisher, president, and editor—at the Nashville paper. He goes on to say in the paper's advertising policy guidelines: "It is in the mutual interest of the staffs of each department to religiously respect that line of separation."

The majority of publishers say that this line demarcating church from state shall not be erased. To do so, they say, would be to commit censorship. Eugene Patterson of the *St. Petersburg Times* wrote:

> It's a free country. A newspaper that chooses not to print news or lawful advertising simply because it editorially disagrees with the thrust of the information is, in my judgment, blinding a community to what is going on in its midst. A community so blinded has no basis for deciding whether it approves or disapproves. The newspaper has presumed not simply to recommend standards editorially; it has decided it will enforce its predilections on others by censoring reality.

In a private memorandum in 1985 to Pat Vander Meer, publisher of *The Progressive*, Erwin Knoll, the magazine's editor, used arguments similar to those advanced by Eugene Patterson:

> We abhor censorship in all of its many forms. We've paid a heavy price, at times, for taking that position—e.g., for defending the free-speech rights of Nazis and Klansmen—but I believe we can take much pride in never having compromised the principle.
> The magazine's advertising policy should be considered in that context— that is, our commitment to promoting the broadest possible freedom of expression. . . . I am convinced that we should *never* reject an ad because we disagree with or disapprove of the individual or organization sponsoring the ad, or because we have political objections to the content. There is no reason at all to shield *The Progressive's* readers from ideas—or, for that matter, from products—that we find troublesome, unappealing, unfortunate, or just plain wrong. If we were to decide, for example, that an ad placed by a group like Feminists for Life of America must be excluded from the magazine, would we also be obliged to exclude an ad for a book setting forth the Feminists for Life position? Would we then have to screen all books and magazines advertising in *The Progressive* to make sure they are politically "correct"?

As compelling as these arguments seem, the failure to breach the Chinese wall, or to cross the divide between church and state, leads to gaps of consistency and logic.

John Hechinger, president of Hechinger Co., a chain of hardware stores, recently wrote a long, reflective letter to the

Washington Post asking why the *Post* accepts handgun advertisements and *Newsweek* (which is owned by the *Post's* parent company) accepts advertisements from the National Rifle Association. Hechinger recalled that after the assassination of John F. Kennedy, he ordered the one store in his chain that sold guns to stop doing so. He did so at the urging of Russell Wiggins, then editor of the *Post.* Hechinger said:

> It is all right to claim there is a Great Wall between the editorial pages and the advertising pages and to claim the necessity to maintain free access by any organization or any cause to the advertising pages. But I am sure that the *Post* and *Newsweek* have set up limitations regarding pornography or extreme political positions that they use to refuse certain advertising submissions that may contain offensive material. Consequently, I ask: Why isn't this screening applied to the acceptance of any type of gun advertising? Further, why isn't this applied to the NRA, which has continuously attempted, and is at this very moment attempting, to gut the already weak handgun laws of this country and which always takes extreme positions, even to the point of objecting to the prohibition of the sale of the "cop-killer bullet," an armor-piercing horror to our nation's law enforcement community.

Hechinger's letter was printed several days after Sam Zagoria, the newspaper's ombudsman, had suggested that the paper voluntarily refrain from accepting cigarette advertising. There was no published response either to Hechinger's letter or to Zagoria's suggestion (even though one high-ranking editor of the paper did submit Zagoria's column for a journalism prize, saying he came "down hard on the media and on his own newspaper"). A few days before Hechinger's letter appeared, Donald E. Graham, the publisher of the *Post,* was interviewed in his paper in connection with a story about smoking. "Our policy is," he said, "we allow advertising of lawful products within certain well-defined limits."

The Costs of Maintaining the Wall

Ultimately, I think, the failure to make distinctions—not on every advertisement certainly, but on a special few—damages the credibility of publishing enterprises.

"To label all judgment over advertising as 'censorship' is to ignore the subtleties," Edward D. Miller, then executive editor of the *Allentown* (Pennsylvania) *Call-Chronicle,* wrote in 1977. He went on to say:

> There's a significant difference between applying standards to advertising and exercising what most would accept to be "censorship." Screening ad

> copy is no more censorship than editing reporter's copy. You set standards and apply judgments based on those standards.
>
> To me the issue is simple. That a person has a right to operate a legal business does not obligate me to help him make a profit by sharing the credibility of my newspaper. Obviously, this is a freedom with great potential for abuse, but that potential is not reason enough to erode the freedom.

For right reasons and wrong ones, newspapers leave out news all the time. In practice, for responsible reasons and for arbitrary ones, they reject advertisements. Many publishers say they feel so strongly about certain issues—escort services, term paper mills, the Ku Klux Klan, coffee or tea—that they are prepared to lose some advertising revenue.

I am not saying that publishers should reject advertisements indiscriminately. Theoretically, publishers print news and lawful advertising even though they disagree with it. Practically, though, much more editorial copy is rejected from a newspaper than advertising copy. It is rejected because it does not strike editors as news, because it does not fit into the allotted space, or because it is dull.

If publishers view themselves as amoral conveyors of advertisements, this permits those who can pay to have greater access to the columns of a newspaper than those who cannot pay. Therefore, commercial speech enjoys a preference that is not legally intended.

You wish the world to know you have been promoted. This is "news" to you, your family, your friends, your competitors. You think it is front-page news. But it is not news to the editors of *The New York Times*. They ignore the press release that the press agent whom you hired sent them. The newspaper has space to publish perhaps only one of any one hundred such items. But your promotion is welcome news to the advertising department of the same newspaper so long as you accompany your advertising copy with a check. For $360, *The Times* will gladly print—on page one, at that—what you wish them to say about your promotion in two lines of copy. To be sure, this is at the bottom of the page, in slightly different (and smaller) typeface from the standard news columns. It is labeled advertisement, and therefore lacks the imprimatur of the news columns. But these are minor reservations, given the appearance of your name on the front page. You want people to say: "Gee, I saw your promotion was mentioned in *The Times* today."

Say, Philip Morris writes a letter—or sends a press release—suggesting that the AMA is all wet. The newspaper may or may not publish it. The reporter or editor may feel it is a wishy-washy statement, or ungrammatical, or too polemical. The letter or release may have come in too late to be published. Or another company may have expressed these thoughts more cogently. It is the First Amendment right of the papers not to publish the item. But if Philip Morris agrees to *pay* to have its letter or press release published as an advertisement, most papers and magazines apparently feel they are left with no choice, under a contorted understanding of freedom of the press, but to publish it.

What happens, then, is that in failing to monitor certain advertising, publications are often giving a superior claim to commercial speech. They wind up rejecting editorial copy, but not advertising copy. I am not proposing forced access to the news columns. It is the well-established right of newspapers *not* to carry Philip Morris's press release, and I do not think that should be disturbed. What I am proposing is that publications, in very limited circumstances, exercise as much diligence—or arbitrariness—about what goes into the advertising columns as what goes into the news columns. This would permit them to reject advertisements for products they would deplore on their editorial pages.

4 / Drawing Lines

There are others in the USA who would ban ads for other legal products: liquor, guns, toy tanks, movies, even skimpy lingerie. The list is endless.

—Editorial, *USA Today*, December 19, 1985

Steering a consistent course between editorial integrity and commercial survival is treacherous. One of the most thoughtful exchanges about this problem appeared nearly a decade ago, in 1977, in the pages of *The New Yorker* and the *Columbia Journalism Review*. The discussion, which centered on cigarettes, has implications for all products. The debate began with a long "Talk of The Town" item, which underscored the print media's growing appetite for cigarette advertisements and the fact that "the press has been paying very little attention to the issue of cigarettes and public health."

The New Yorker specifically criticized the magazine published by Columbia University's Graduate School of Journalism: "Currently, even the *Columbia Journalism Review*, which supposedly exists for the purpose of subjecting the reporting standards of the American press to critical examination, has been helping to sustain itself financially by running full-page color ads for cigarettes, and it seems to us that when this happens, something is really awry."

In a brisk rejoinder, Edward Barrett, publisher of the *Review*, pointed out that its policy was under study (the magazine subsequently decided to continue to accept cigarette advertising) and raised these "troubling" questions:

How does a magazine's dedication to free speech stack up against its assuming the role of protecting readers from ads for a product which the ads clearly label as a health hazard?

. . .Could we justify rejecting cigarette ads but publishing liquor ads, as does *The New Yorker?* Or should you and we either accept both, as do most publications, or reject both, as do the *Reader's Digest, The Christian Science Monitor* and *Seventeen?*

. . . Isn't a much more fundamental issue involved?. . . Are we to take it upon ourselves to decide from which legal products to protect our readers?. . . Yet if publications once start the process of selecting ads, might it lead some into the treacherous area of excluding advertising for any product subject to abuse and ultimately any product, book, play or idea of which they happen to disapprove?

In a long letter to the *Review,* Melvin Mencher, a feisty professor at the graduate school of journalism, derided the argument that "the *Review* is dedicated to free speech, that it has no right to 'decide from which legal products to protect our readers.'" That defense, he said, "is reminiscent of the statement of publishers in the thirties that paying newsboys a minimum wage would threaten freedom of the press. I am sure Mr. Dooley's comment does not apply here, but whenever pieties of the kind used to defend cigarette manufacturers are injected into discussions about the press I'm reminded of what Finley Peter Dunne had him say: 'Th' American nation in th' Sixth Ward is a fine people. They love th' eagle on th' back iv a dollar.'"

What, Mencher asked, "is the moral use of the advertising columns of the *Review?* To allow any and all advertisers their say? I don't think any major newspaper in the country does that. The advertising departments of newspapers are no different from the editorial sections in this respect. Every day in newsrooms and offices decisions are made about what to run in news and advertising columns. Journalism at all levels is the art of knowing what to leave out. . . ."

Mencher then turned to the critical issue of access. The *Review's* reluctance to make decisions about advertising, he said, effectively "grants the advertiser—that is, those who have the funds to buy space—the same right of access as the candidate of a minority party, the dissenter on the city council. Not only does it blur the line between access to the free columns of the newspaper or magazine and the paid space, it states that journalists are incapable of making judgments, of drawing lines."

In a brief last word closing off the lengthy debate, Barrett said: "The *Review,* like the overwhelming majority of American publications, would not presume to 'protect' its readers from

advertising of products whose sale is still fully legal—particularly when the ads contain a clear and prominent warning."

The editors of the *Columbia Journalism Review* were concerned with the slippery slope. So are the editors of *USA Today*
who worry about toy tanks and skimpy lingerie, and so are the
editors of the *Louisville Times* who wrote in reaction to the AMA
proposal:

> Certainly newspapers have benefited from cigarette ads; if the kind of ban
> that the AMA seeks were imposed, we would feel its effects. But so would
> millions of Americans whose right to receive information about legal prod-
> ucts would be jeopardized. Cigarettes aren't the only products that endanger
> lives or safety. Liquor, when consumed to excess, is dangerous. Chain saws,
> lawn mowers, shotguns and all sorts of mechanical equipment, if improperly
> operated, can jeopardize safety.

The Slippery Slope

Somehow, the argument goes, if publishers reject advertising
for one type of product, they may well exclude advertisements
for books, plays, and ideas that they happen to disapprove of.
This reasoning by absurd analogy belittles the role of journalists.
When it comes to advertising, they are capable of making
reasonable and intelligent judgments, just as they are able to
decide what stories to run each day and where to play them.

In 1985, at congressional hearings on whether advertisements
alerting consumers to the harmful effects of alcohol should be
required, however, speaker after speaker referred to the "slippery
slope" that would be greased, to the "Pandora's box" that would
be opened, to the parade of horribles that would inevitably
stampede right-thinking people if such a policy were adopted.

"If counterads are to be mandated, where does one draw the
line in terms of products subjected to counterads?" asked
Representative Timothy Wirth (D.-Colorado), who had called the
hearings. "What about ads for food products, drugs or cosmetics?
If we start down such a path with beer and wine ads, where does
it stop?" He supplied no answers.

Another speaker, Donald B. Shea, president of the United
States Brewers Association, argued that it would be wrong to
extend the Fairness Doctrine to the advertising of beer or any
other commercial product:

> Excessive consumption of soft drinks, coffee, tea, eggs, milk, red meat, sugar
> and numerous other foods is believed by some to create various health prob-

lems. The artificial sweeteners in soft drinks, for example, raise health issues that might be deemed to warrant responsive advertising. Similarly, automobiles are associated with highway deaths, gasoline with air pollution and aerosols with other environmental problems. . . .The simple fact is that no line can fairly be drawn around any product or group of products, and any decision to open the advertising of one product to the Fairness Doctrine should open all advertising of all products to the doctrine.

Only John Banzhaf III, who had successfully argued nearly twenty years earlier that the Fairness Doctrine be applied to cigarette advertising, presented a clear distinction between cigarettes and alcohol and most other products. "They are," he said, "so far as I know, the only products which, both by law and custom, are restricted to adult consumption."

Banzhaf advocated a "graduated response" to the regulation of possibly harmful products: "To leave private enterprise free to develop and promote new products, including drugs, food additives, and substances which may affect the environment, the government must be able to make a graduated response to the danger as evidence against the product accumulates. This might include limitations on unsubstantiated claims, prescribed warnings in some or all ads, a ban on ads in some media (e.g., publications directed to children, restricting advertising to medical journals, etc.) or a total ban on all advertising."

Taking a Stand

To hear many publishers tell it, a voluntary ban on one product—like cigarettes—would unavoidably lead to the exclusion of advertisements for other products: first cigarettes, then maybe toy tanks or lawn mowers. They often seem to lack confidence in their own common sense.

Yet, publishers have rejected advertisements for all sorts of reasonable—and arbitrary—reasons. Occasionally, publishers have rejected advertisements as a matter of social conscience. That is what the publisher of the paper in New London was doing when he rejected advertisements for "Happy Hours." And, of course, he is not the only publisher to have demonstrated social responsibility.

In the late 1960s, at least two major publishers—*The Boston Globe* and *The New York Times*—decided to forgo advertising revenues at the very time when, with tobacco advertising going off television, they could have reaped large benefits. In a 1969 editorial, *The New York Times* explained that it was adopting a new policy, under which manufacturers would have to include health warnings in order to advertise. This was not then required by law as it is today. In its editorial, *The Times* stressed it was taking "voluntary action." The tobacco companies retaliated and withdrew their advertising from *The Times* for several years, resuming business only when such warnings became mandatory.

On September 4, 1969, the American Tobacco Company took out a full page advertisement in *The Times*. The headline read: WHY WE'RE DROPPING THE NEW YORK TIMES. The text of the advertisement began: "We offered to take our ads off TV and radio because of the claim that those media unavoidably reach large numbers of children." It ended:

> In 1884, the *New York Times* said: "The decadence of Spain began when the Spaniards adopted cigarettes and if this pernicious practice obtains among adult Americans the ruin of the Republic is close at hand. . . ."
> We think the *New York Times* was wrong in 1884. We think it is wrong in 1969.

In May 1969, the management of *The Boston Globe* took an even stronger stand, announcing that the newspaper would no longer accept cigarette advertising "because accumulated medical evidence has indicated that cigarette smoking is hazardous to health."

Generally, though, the situation was as Thomas Whiteside described in *The New Yorker:*

> As for the newspaper publishers, no matter what their editorials might have been saying about smoking and health, or how dispassionately they had viewed the plight of the broadcasters faced with the issue of smoking and health, they showed, on the whole, that they had no intention of eliminating cigarette advertising or even of turning away further revenues that might follow the proposed cutoffs of cigarette commercials from the airwaves.

Only a few newspapers had followed the example of *The Boston Globe,* and most changed their minds after the FTC established regulations in 1972 requiring all print cigarette advertising to include a "clear and conspicuous health warning."

In 1974, five years after it had banned cigarette advertisements, *The Boston Globe* announced in an editorial that it would resume accepting them:

> When *The Globe* dropped cigarette advertising, it did so knowing that a large amount of advertising income was involved, but out of the convic-

tion that cigarette smoking is dangerous to one's health and that therefore cigarette advertising was against the public interest.. . .

The Globe has reconsidered its position and has decided there is a larger question here—one of access, a responsibility to its public to allow the varying voices of the community appropriate access to its advertising space.

The paid columns of a newspaper are somewhat like a freight train, available to carry all products, the movement of which is not forbidden by law. If the power to restrict the freight is used unilaterally and extensively and indiscriminately, may not society begin to wonder whether such a life-and-death grip on economic activity should be conferred on a purely private and perhaps even elite group? And should a newspaper have the right to impose its view by economic sanctions? We think not.

The about-face made by these papers is now total. In 1985, The Boston Globe did not editorialize on the AMA's proposal for a cigarette advertising ban. Nor was there any editorial comment in The New York Times, which has editorialized against the harms of smoking for more than two decades (in May 1986, for instance, it called smoking "a proven health risk"). No columnists wrote about it in The Times. There were no op-ed pieces, and only a couple of letters appeared.

Earlier in 1985, The Times had published an article on its op-ed page written by George Gitlitz, a vascular surgeon from Binghamton, New York and a gadfly of the cigarette industry. Gitlitz asked why "newspapers, including The New York Times, persist in running" cigarette advertisements. Advertising cigarettes, he said, "isn't a crime. It's just wrong. The effect, in the practical world of the marketplace, is no different from newspapers renting airstrips for planes carrying cocaine."

One letter was printed in response to his article. It derided Gitlitz for belonging to "My Brother's Keeper Lodge." The author of the letter was Guy Smith IV, the vice president for corporate affairs of Philip Morris, who, over the past couple of years, has had a remarkably easy time getting his letters published in the country's newspapers.*

The Times did not publicly respond to the doctor's question

---

*Several newspapers, including the St. Louis Post-Dispatch and the Los Angeles Times, ran a letter Smith wrote after the AMA proposal was announced; the Nashville Banner ran it as an op-ed piece. Smith wrote: "They tried to silence Thomas Paine. Thank God they failed. They tried to silence Thomas Jefferson. Thank God they failed. They tried to silence Susan B. Anthony. Thank God they failed. They tried to silence Martin Luther King. In death his voice is only better heard. To be sure I cannot stand with these historical giants. But my freedom to be heard is not less than theirs. And now the American Medical Association wants to silence me. I want a second opinion!"

of why it runs cigarette advertisements. Indeed, *The Times*, which voluntarily lived without cigarette advertising revenues in the early 1970s, seems to have become more aggressive in seeking them these days, and one of the first things The New York Times Company did after purchasing the *Sarasota Herald-Tribune* late in 1982 was to reverse that paper's long-standing policy of refusing cigarette advertising.

The *Times* has energetically solicited tobacco advertisers in an important trade publication, the *U.S. Tobacco and Candy Journal*. The salutation of one recent advertisement was: "Lifestyles are made, not born." The text read: "Three million weekday readers and four million Sunday readers *believe* in the trend-setting advertising they see in its atmosphere of quality and credibility." (emphasis in original)

That advertisement, Joseph A. Califano, Jr., the former secretary of health, education and welfare, told me, "was the crassest thing I ever saw."

In his recent book, *America's Health Care Revolution, Who Lives? Who Dies? Who Pays?*, Califano condemns publications that "rail against the dangers of smoking and attack the hypocrisy of a government policy that urges us not to smoke yet subsidizes farmers to grow tobacco." These same newspapers and magazines, he wrote, "are just as hypocritical: they not only run cigarette ads, they hustle to get them, and they refuse to carry ads alerting people to the dangers of smoking."

Califano, now a Washington lawyer, continued: "Newspapers and magazines that hawk cigarettes should not be able to camouflage their avarice by talking fatuous First Amendment rights."

In 1984, the Medical Society of the State of New York passed a resolution directing the president of the group to write to publishers of the leading newspapers and periodicals based in New York to urge them to refuse advertising for cigarettes. Eighteen publishers were contacted; only six replied. One of those, *The New Yorker*, had refused to accept cigarette advertising since shortly after the 1964 surgeon general's report. The others declined to change their policies.

Making Decisions

Those publishers who continue to accept cigarette advertisements argue that readers are sophisticated enough to know of the dangers of harmful products such as cigarettes. I submit that publishers are smart enough to distinguish between inherently harmful products and those that are not.

It is not possible to formulate sweeping rules. Nor must the exclusion of advertisements of one product inevitably lead to the exclusion of others.

Decisions about advertising must be made on a case-by-case basis. After muckraking against abortion clinics, the *Chicago Sun-Times* would have been hypocritical to continue to accept advertising dollars from these clinics. It acted responsibly in cutting these advertisements off.

Publishers need to be reminded that by forgoing revenues, their publications can make an unambiguous and valuable social statement that can have as much impact on a community as a hard-hitting investigative story or as an act of corporate philanthropy.